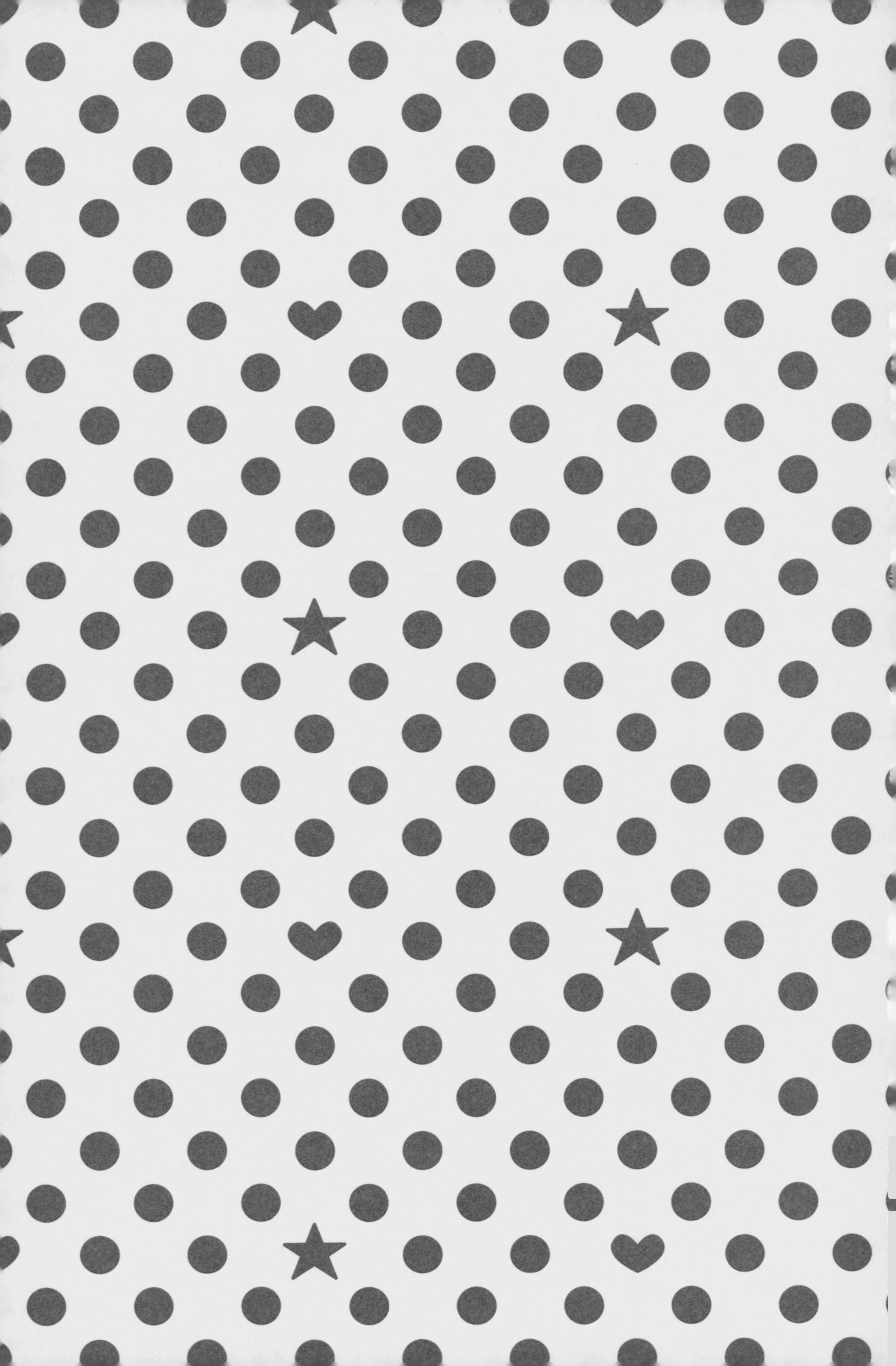

Aggretsuko™

meet her friends

I CANNOT COMPETE WITH YOU, PROTEIN

WRITTEN BY Cat Farris ILLUSTRATED BY Lisa DuBois

COLORS BY Andrew Dalhouse

FENNEKO'S GRAND PLAN

WRITTEN BY Arielle Jovellanos

ILLUSTRATED AND COLORS BY Diigii Daguna

THE GOLF BETWEEN US

WRITTEN BY James Asmus ILLUSTRATED BY Megan Huang

COLORS BY Andrew Dalhouse

ALL PAGES LETTERED BY Crank!

REGULAR COVER BY Phil Murphy

Aggretsuko™

meet her friends

ONI PRESS

AN ONI PRESS PUBLICATION

DESIGNED BY SARAH ROCKWELL AND KATE Z. STONE **EDITED BY** SARAH GAYDOS AND ROBERT MEYERS

SPECIAL THANKS TO
CINDY SUZUKI, JEFF PARKER, MARJORIE SANTOS, SUZAN ZHANG, SUSAN TRAN, RENEE HAMMER, ELLEN IZYKOWSKI, AND LINH FORSE FOR THEIR INVALUABLE ASSISTANCE.

onipress.com

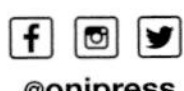

@onipress

lionforge.com

@lionforge

PUBLISHED BY ONI-LION FORGE PUBLISHING GROUP, LLC
James Lucas Jones, president & publisher **Sarah Gaydos**, editor in chief **Charlie Chu**, e.v.p. of creative & business development **Brad Rooks**, director of operations **Amber O'Neill**, special projects manager **Margot Wood**, director of marketing & sales **Devin Funches**, sales & marketing manager **Katie Sainz**, marketing manager **Tara Lehmann**, publicist **Troy Look**, director of design & production **Kate Z. Stone**, senior graphic designer **Sonja Synak**, graphic designer **Hilary Thompson**, graphic designer **Sarah Rockwell**, graphic designer **Angie Knowles**, digital prepress lead **Vincent Kukua**, digital prepress technician **Jasmine Amiri**, senior editor **Shawna Gore**, senior editor **Amanda Meadows**, senior editor **Robert Meyers**, senior editor, licensing **Desiree Rodriguez**, editor **Grace Scheipeter**, editor **Zack Soto**, editor **Chris Cerasi**, editorial coordinator **Steve Ellis**, vice president of games **Ben Eisner**, game developer **Michelle Nguyen**, executive assistant **Jung Lee**, logistics coordinator **Joe Nozemack**, publisher emeritus

sanrio.com
@sanrio
@aggretsuko
aggretsuko
@aggretsuko
aggretsuko

SIL-34865

First Edition: MARCH 2021
REGULAR ISBN 978-1-62010-877-2
eISBN 978-1-62010-878-6

Printing numbers:
1 3 5 7 9 10 8 6 4 2

Library of Congress Control Number 2020940920

Printed in Canada.

ガ
平

OASIS KARAOKE.
激安
カラオケ
受付2階
RAAAAAHHH!
TWISTING AND CONTORTING!
CAN HARDLY KEEP MY BALANCE!
I FEEL LIKE A FOOL IN THOSE POSITIONS!
TO HELL WITH YOUR YOGA!!

AH, I'M COMPLETELY WIPED.

TELL ME AGAIN WHY WE DECIDED TO GO OUT FOR KARAOKE AFTER YOGA CLASS?

POOR RETSUKO. CAN'T KEEP UP, *HUH?* MAYBE YOU NEED SOME...

PROTEIN!

HA HA HA
HA HA

THAT'S PRETTY GOOD, GORI. BUT I THINK IT'S ACTUALLY MORE LIKE...

PROTEIN!
BWAHAHAHA!
HA-HA, GOOD ONE, WASHIMI. BUT DON'T YOU THINK IT'S A BIT MORE LIKE...
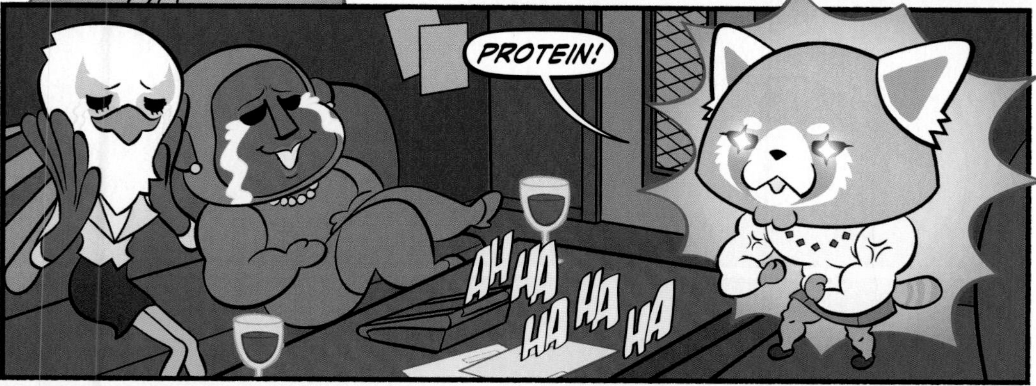
PROTEIN!
AH HA
HA HA HA

AH HAHA... HAA...

OH!

WASHIMI, GORI, YOU'VE BOTH BEEN TAKING YOGA CLASSES AT THAT STUDIO LONGER THAN I HAVE.
DO YOU KNOW ANYTHING ABOUT THE INSTRUCTOR?
HE'S JUST SO...

WELL...

HIMSELF?

YES! EXACTLY! THERE HAS TO BE A STORY BEHIND IT ALL, DON'T YOU THINK?

HMMM, INDEED.
COME TO THINK OF IT, I DO BELIEVE I OVERHEARD TWO OF THE OTHER WOMEN IN CLASS TALKING ABOUT HIM A WHILE BACK.
THEY WERE SAYING THAT HE USED TO BE AN EVIL YOGA INSTRUCTOR, WITH A REPUTATION FOR CRUELTY THAT WAS KNOWN WORLDWIDE.

"HE USED HIS YOGA KNOWLEDGE TO BRING ABOUT INCREDIBLE SUFFERING.
"HE SPREAD MISERY FAR AND WIDE.
"UNTIL..."

NOOOOOOOOOOOO!!

"HE WAS STRUCK BY ALL THE MISERY HE'D CAUSED AND HORRIFIED BY HIS ACTIONS.
HUK
WAAAAAAAAA!
"FROM THAT DAY FORWARD, HE VOWED TO USE HIS YOGA STRENGTH ONLY FOR GOOD. HE ALSO TOOK A VOW OF SILENCE, EXCEPT FOR ONE WORD."
PROTEIN.

AT LEAST, THAT WAS WHAT I HEARD.
HO HO HO! IS THAT WHAT YOU HEARD?
WOW.
THAT'S WHAT I JUST SAID, YES.
WELL.
THAT'S A RIDICULOUS STORY. WHO WOULD BELIEVE IT? I HAVE IT ON GOOD AUTHORITY THAT OUR YOGA INSTRUCTOR IS ACTUALLY AN ALIEN.
UHHHH...
HE WAS SENT TO EARTH BY HIS PARENTS RIGHT BEFORE HIS HOME PLANET WAS DESTROYED.
KADOOOM
SHOOOOOOW

TUMP!
"HE WAS FOUND AND ADOPTED BY A BODYBUILDER AND A YOGA INSTRUCTOR.
"THEY RAISED HIM AS IF HE WAS THEIR OWN.
"THEY TAUGHT HIM EVERYTHING THEY KNEW.
"THEY DISCOVERED THAT EARTH PROTEIN GIVES HIM TEN TIMES THE STRENGTH OF A NORMAL PERSON."
PROTEIN!

"HE SOON DISCOVERED HE
COULD ACHIEVE AMAZING
FEATS OF STRENGTH!"

"HE MAY SEEM LIKE A MILD-MANNERED YOGA INSTRUCTOR...
平和
"...WHO IS ONLY OBSESSED WITH PROTEIN...
PROTEIN!
PROTEIN!
PROTEIN!
"...BUT IT'S REALLY JUST A COVER...
HELP!
"...AS HIS TRUE IDENTITY OF
FEARLESS YOGA SUPERHERO

AH HA HAH HAH HAH!
HAH HEE HEE HEE!

MY STORY WAS UNBELIEVABLE? OH, GORI!

HAHAHAHAHA!

IT'S TRUE! WHY ARE YOU LAUGHING?!

...I ALWAYS LIKED TO IMAGINE THAT HE'S THE WAY HE IS BECAUSE HE WAS CURSED BY A WITCH.

WHAT?!

YOU SEE, BEFORE WE KNEW HIM, HE WAS MADLY IN LOVE WITH A BEAUTIFUL GIRL!

"BUT HE WAS SO SCRAWNY.
700
850
500
"THE WOMAN HE LOVED DIDN'T EVEN *NOTICE* HIM!
食べ物を得た!
"HE WAS DEVASTATED."

"SO HE WENT TO SEE A WITCH IN THE HOPES THAT SHE WOULD HAVE A WAY TO MAKE THE GIRL FALL IN LOVE WITH HIM.
"THE WITCH TOLD HIM SHE KNEW JUST THE THING TO HELP.
"SHE PROMISED TO GIVE HIM A REALLY BUFF BODY THAT NO ONE COULD *POSSIBLY* IGNORE!
"BUT IN RETURN, HE'D HAVE TO GIVE HER HIS VOICE, WHICH WAS STRANGELY SULTRY FOR SUCH A SCRAWNY GUY!
"ALL HE WOULD BE ABLE TO SAY WAS '*PROTEIN*,' BUT IF HE COULD GET THE GIRL TO FALL FOR HIM, THE WITCH PROMISED TO GIVE HIM BACK HIS VOICE. SO HE AGREED AND THE DEAL WAS MADE."

"HE WAS SO CONFIDENT THAT HIS NEW BODY WOULD FINALLY GET HIS LOVE'S ATTENTION.
"BUT IT TURNED OUT THAT THE WITCH STOLE HIS SULTRY VOICE AND USED IT TO MAKE THE GIRL FALL IN LOVE WITH *HER*!"

"UNFORTUNATELY, HE WASN'T ABLE TO TELL ANYONE WHAT HAD HAPPENED TO HIM.
PROTEIN!
"WITH HIS LOVE LOST TO HIM, HE DECIDED TO OPEN A YOGA STUDIO.
SOLD
"THAT WAY, HE COULD HELP OTHERS GET BUFF BODIES WITHOUT HAVING TO MAKE A SHADY DEAL WITH A WITCH!"
ヨガ
平和

YOU READ TOO MANY FAIRY TALES.
SWEET, INNOCENT RETSUKO.

I STILL FEEL LIKE MY STORY IS ACCURATE.

NO WAY! MY STORY IS RIGHT. YOU WON'T GET ME TO CHANGE MY MIND, WASHIMI.

UH, MAYB--
NOK
NOK
NOK

PLEASE EXCUSE ME! THE TIME ON YOUR RESERVATION IS-- *OH!*

AH... SORRY TO INTERRUPT, BUT YOUR, *AH*, TIME IS UP.
THANK YOU FOR SINGING WITH US?

THANK YOU.

206
HONESTLY, GORI. SUPERHEROES AREN'T REAL.
I REFUSE TO BELIEVE THAT ANYONE WHO DOES YOGA COULD EVER BE EVIL.
LIFE ISN'T A COMIC BOOK, YOU KNOW.
I JUST THINK IT SOUNDS ROMANTIC...

206
204
YOU'RE NOT LISTENING!
I'M JUST SAYING!

204
206
206
PROTEIN!

受付
営業中
karac
酒場
小節
The End

烈

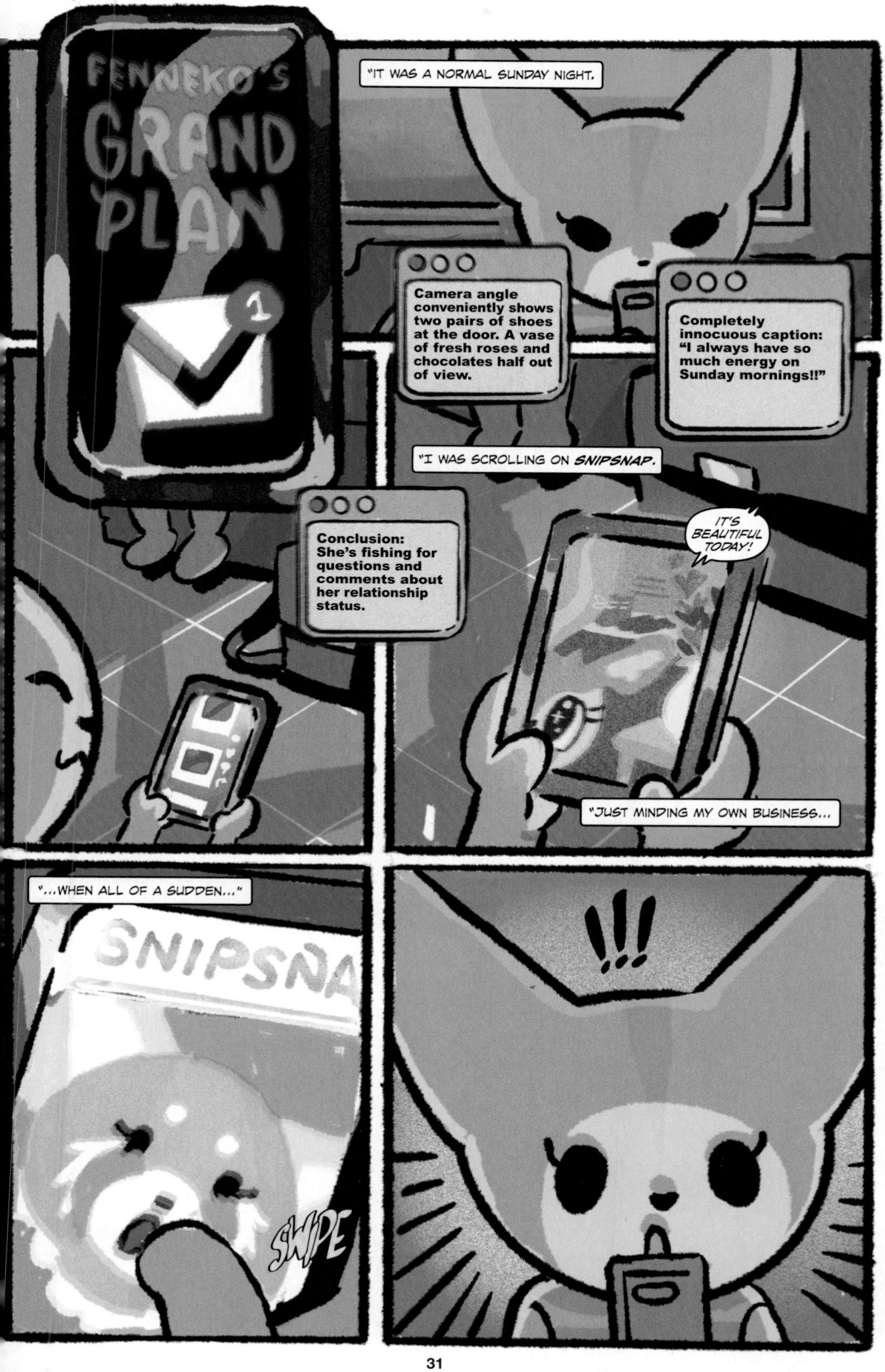

FENNEKO'S GRAND PLAN

"IT WAS A NORMAL SUNDAY NIGHT.

Camera angle conveniently shows two pairs of shoes at the door. A vase of fresh roses and chocolates half out of view.

Completely innocuous caption: "I always have so much energy on Sunday mornings!!"

Conclusion: She's fishing for questions and comments about her relationship status.

"I WAS SCROLLING ON *SNIPSNAP*.

IT'S BEAUTIFUL TODAY!

"JUST MINDING MY OWN BUSINESS...

HAHAH
HAHAHAHAH

HEY, FOR ¥600, WHAT'S TWO PLUS TWO?

UH, UH, UH...!!!

...TWENTY-TWO?

WAIT, WAIT, PLAY IT AGAIN!

YOU *GUYS!!*

OKAY, *UH*, CUT IT OUT, FENNEKO.

WOW, RETSUKO, ONE MILLION VIEWS... ***HAHAHAHAHA!***
HOW WAS I SUPPOSED TO KNOW HE WAS SOME FAMOUS INTERNET GUY?
I MEAN, IT'S KIND OF COOL, RIGHT? IT'S NOT EVERY DAY I COME INTO WORK AND MEET A VIRAL SENSATION.

I GUESS IT'S COOL IF YOU IGNORE THE BAD SIDE OF IT. A LOT OF VIRAL CELEBRITIES GET FIRED FROM THEIR REAL JOBS. COMPANIES HATE BAD PUBLICITY AND DON'T WANT ROGUE EMPLOYEES GIVING THEM A NEGATIVE IMAGE OVER SOME STUPID INTERNET THING. IT ACTUALLY WOULDN'T BE CRAZY IF RETSUKO GOT FIRED OVER THIS.
NO WAY.
YEAH. I READ AN ARTICLE ABOUT IT.

WAIT. ***FIRED?!***
YOU'RE A PROFESSIONAL ACCOUNTANT. YOU SAID TWO PLUS TWO EQUALS TWENTY-TWO. IN FRONT OF ONE MILLION PEOPLE.
DON'T LISTEN TO HER, RETSUKO. IT'S JUST A SILLY APP FOR KIDS.
BESIDES, YOUR BOSS WOULD ***REALLY*** NEED TO BE AN ASSHOLE TO FIRE YOU FOR A LITTLE THING LIKE THAT.

YOU HAVE BROUGHT WORLDWIDE SHAME ONTO THIS ACCOUNTING DEPARTMENT!!
HOW DAAAARE YOOOOUUUU!!
BUT

YOU KNOW WHAT? YOU'RE RIGHT!
IT'S NOT LIKE TON'S SPENDING HIS PRECIOUS DAYS OFF ON SNIPSNAP.

SO...

LATELY, I'VE BEEN COMING HOME FROM WORK COMPLETELY EXHAUSTED.
LATE
I GO TO WORK EACH DAY WITH A SMILE ON MY FACE, ONLY TO BE GIVEN NEVER-ENDING PILES OF PAPERWORK.
EVERYONE EXPECTS ME TO DO EVERYTHING FOR THEM WITH NOTHING IN RETURN.

YET... THERE IS *ONE* SAVING GRACE TO MY DAY.
BUT YOU DON'T EVEN *DO* ANYTHING!!
NOT WORK

THE *BONE APPETIZER* COOKING CHANNEL.
EVEN WHEN I DON'T FEEL LIKE COOKING ANYTHING MYSELF, I JUST TURN ON MY TV AND WATCH THESE PROFESSIONAL CHEFS MAKE THEIR DELECTABLE SWEETS AND DELICIOUS ENTREES.
ALL MY TROUBLES MELT AWAY.

UM. THAT'S GREAT, ANAI.
YES. IT *IS* GREAT. THEY'RE EVEN HOLDING A SPECIAL FOOD FESTIVAL TWO WEEKENDS FROM NOW. I BOUGHT MY TICKET MONTHS AGO.

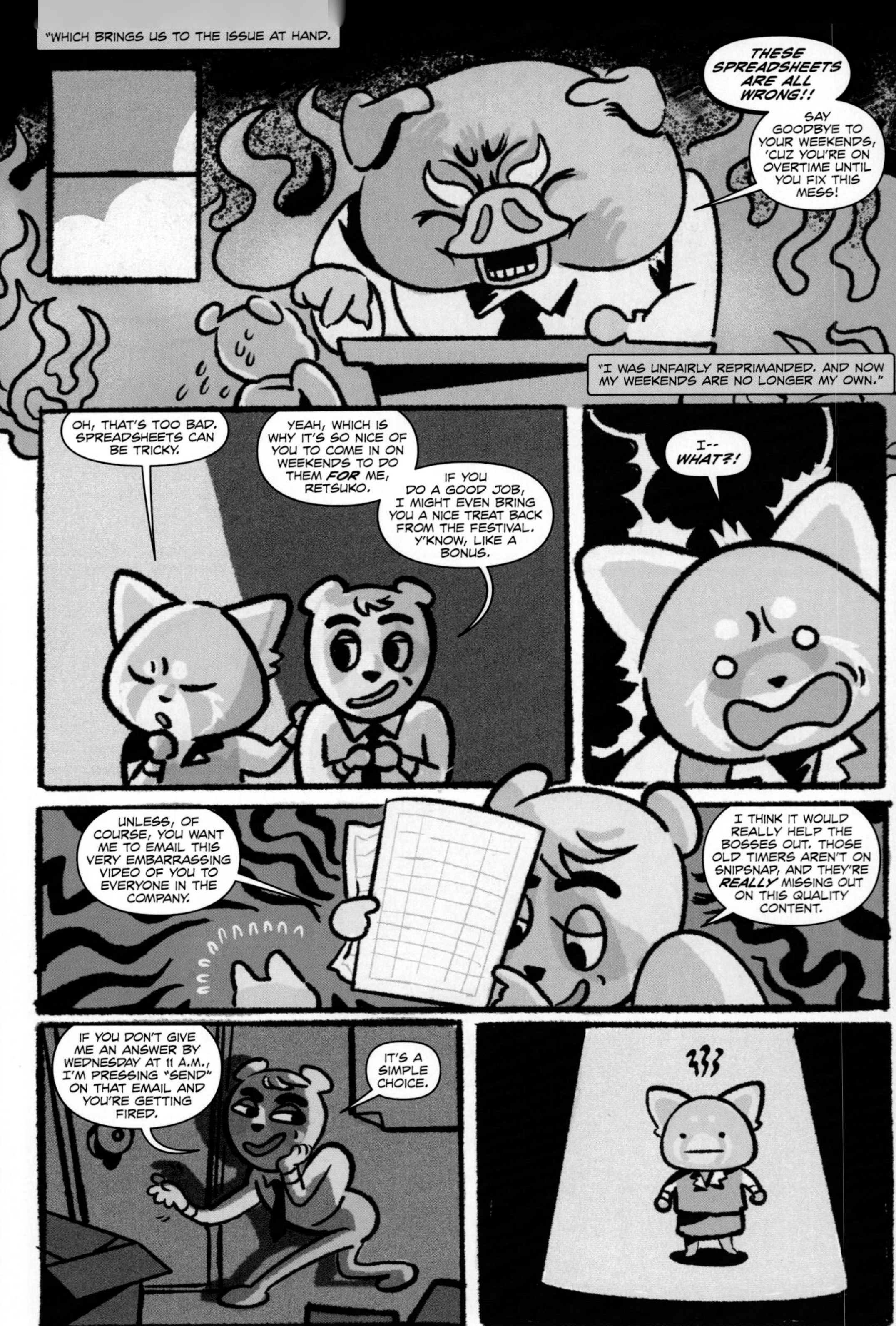
"WHICH BRINGS US TO THE ISSUE AT HAND.
THESE SPREADSHEETS ARE ALL WRONG!!
SAY GOODBYE TO YOUR WEEKENDS, 'CUZ YOU'RE ON OVERTIME UNTIL YOU FIX THIS MESS!
"I WAS UNFAIRLY REPRIMANDED. AND NOW MY WEEKENDS ARE NO LONGER MY OWN."
OH, THAT'S TOO BAD. SPREADSHEETS CAN BE TRICKY.
YEAH, WHICH IS WHY IT'S SO NICE OF YOU TO COME IN ON WEEKENDS TO DO THEM *FOR* ME, RETSUKO.
IF YOU DO A GOOD JOB, I MIGHT EVEN BRING YOU A NICE TREAT BACK FROM THE FESTIVAL. Y'KNOW, LIKE A BONUS.
I-- *WHAT?!*
UNLESS, OF COURSE, YOU WANT ME TO EMAIL THIS VERY EMBARRASSING VIDEO OF YOU TO EVERYONE IN THE COMPANY.
I THINK IT WOULD REALLY HELP THE BOSSES OUT. THOSE OLD TIMERS AREN'T ON SNIPSNAP, AND THEY'RE *REALLY* MISSING OUT ON THIS QUALITY CONTENT.
IF YOU DON'T GIVE ME AN ANSWER BY WEDNESDAY AT 11 A.M., I'M PRESSING "SEND" ON THAT EMAIL AND YOU'RE GETTING FIRED.
IT'S A SIMPLE CHOICE.

THAT LITTLE BRAAAAAAAT!!
HOW DO YOU EVEN MESS UP A SPREADSHEET?! I LEARNED HOW TO DO THEM IN MIDDLE SCHOOOOOL!!
CAN YOU BELIEVE THAT GUY?!
MM-HM.
WELL, THERE GO MY WEEKENDS FOREVER!
MM-HM.
WHAT'S GONNA STOP HIM FROM HOLDING THAT VIDEO OVER MY HEAD EVERY TIME HE WANTS SOMETHING?
MM-HM.
I MEAN, WHAT AM I GONNA DO? JUST BLOCK THE WHOLE COMPANY FROM RECEIVING ANAI'S EMAILS?!
MM-HM.
WAIT A MINUTE! FENNEKO!

YOU'RE, LIKE, AN EXPERT AT THE INTERNET, RIGHT?
HM? YEAH, I GUESS--
YOU HAVE TO HELP ME!! PLEASE?
STOP ANAI?
MUU
Retsuko. Friend in trouble. Best lunch buddy. If she gets fired, work will be boring.
Haida. A sucker who will do anything for Retsuko.
GREEN WEEK
HAIDA
CEO Shachou. Loves themed company events. Capture the King, Get the Power...
I SUPPOSE IT'S POSSIBLE.
BUT WE'RE GOING TO NEED A TEAM.

THANKS FOR MEETING US HERE TODAY.
I KNOW WE ALL ENJOY RETSUKO'S COMPANY AND WOULD HATE TO SEE HER FIRED.
SO THERE'S NO SPECIAL EMPLOYEE-OF-THE-MONTH BUFFET?
SHH!
OOOOO!! THIS IS SO EXCITING!
OH! DO WE GET TO WEAR SPECIAL OUTFITS?
THESE FOLDERS HAVE YOUR INDIVIDUAL MISSION PARAMETERS INSIDE.
DON'T WORRY, RETSUKO. WE'VE GOT THIS UNDER CONTROL.
REALLY, RETSUKO, TWO PLUS TWO EQUALS TWENTY-TWO?!
WHAT ABOUT ME? WHAT SHOULD I DO?
YOU DON'T HAVE TO DO ANYTHING. EXCEPT...
?
EXCEPT?
MAKE SURE ANAI SENDS THAT EMAIL.

TWO DAYS LATER.
THE DAY OF ANAI'S DEADLINE.
FENNEKO! I BET YOU'RE HAVING A HARD TIME WITH THE NEW COMPANY MINDFULNESS INITIATIVE, *HUH?!*

I KNOW YOU LOVE BEING ON YOUR PHONE, SO LOCKING IT UP FOR HOURS MUST BE TORTURE FOR YOU, RIGHT?!
WHEN MR. SHACHOU JUST ***DROPPED*** THIS ON EVERYONE YESTERDAY, I WAS, LIKE, ***"UH-OH!! FENNEKO!!"***

I WAS READING THE PAMPHLET HE GAVE OUT. DID YOU KNOW PRACTICING MINDFULNESS CAN LEAD TO LONGER LIFE SPANS? THAT'S PRETTY COOL! I GUESS NOT BEING ON OUR PHONES MEANS WE CAN HAVE MORE INTIMATE FACE-TO-FACE DISCUSSIONS, JUST LIKE RIGHT NOW, *HUH,* FENNEKO?

WOW, I FEEL LIKE I'VE GOTTEN TO KNOW YOU MUCH BETTER ALREADY!

DING!

KTICKTOCKTICKTO
10:59
EPLY
ALL
SEND
SENT!

URGENT: VIEW ASAP
HM?
BZZZZ
WHAT THE HELL?!
THIS IS SECRETARY WASHIMI OVER THE BUILDING-WIDE EMERGENCY SERVICE SPEAKER. THERE HAS BEEN A MOMENTARY POWER FAILURE IN THE WEST SIDE OF THE BUILDING.
FOR SAFETY PURPOSES, EVERYONE PLEASE MEET AT THE EAST SIDE AUDITORIUM WHILE THE ELECTRICIAN WORKS ON THE ISSUE.

WOMAN ON THE INSIDE
THANK YOU.
EXCELLENT WORK AS EVER, WASHIMI!
THERE *IS* THE ISSUE OF WHAT TO DO WITH EVERYBODY IN THE AUDITORIUM NOW, SIR. IT MAY TAKE A WHILE TO DIAGNOSE THE ELECTRIC PROBLEM. WE CAN'T HAVE THE WHOLE COMPANY DOING NOTHING FOR HOURS.
YOU'RE ABSOLUTELY RIGHT. WHAT IF WE HIRED A MAGICIAN TO--
SLAM
MARKETING DIRECTOR GORI WAS SCHEDULED TO DO A PRESENTATION FOR THE COMPANY TOMORROW, SIR.
I BELIEVE SHE IS READY, AND IT WILL BE A SIMPLE MATTER TO MOVE IT UP TO TODAY. A MUCH BETTER USE OF COMPANY TIME, IS IT NOT?
MY MY, WASHIMI! YOU'VE JUST BEEN FULL OF EXCELLENT IDEAS ALL WEEK!
ESPECIALLY THAT MINDFULNESS INITIATIVE! IT'S BEEN ***WONDERFUL*** FOR THIS OLD BRAIN OF MINE. KEEP UP THE GOOD WORK.

I COMMUTE ALL THE WAY HERE EVERY DAY AND THIS IS THE CRAP I GET?
THE BACK UP
SO... WHAT *IS* MARKETING ANYWAY?
THE DECOY

WOW!! AND WHAT DOES THAT PLIER DO, MR. ELECTRICIAN MAN? YOU MUST BE SO STRONG!
HA-HA. UH. YEAH...
AHEM!
OH, JUST A MINUTE, MR. ELECTRICIAN MAN! WHEN I COME BACK, CAN YOU SHOW ME WHAT HAPPENS WHEN YOU CUT THOSE WIRES? IT'S SOOOOO FASCINATING!
HEY, DID YOU GET MY TEXT? WE SHOULD ALL GET DRINKS LATER!
HOW WOULD I HAVE GOTTEN YOUR TEXT?!
THE SPY
THE MASTER MIND
TOOK YOU LONG ENOUGH.

THE STUDY OF MARKETING, OF COURSE, IS NOT TO BE CONFUSED WITH THE STUDY OF SUPERMARKETS...

YEAH, YEAH, JUST HURRY UP! I'LL WATCH THE DOOR.
PASSWORD
HEY, HAIDA. DID YOU KNOW IN FIFTH GRADE I WON A "FASTEST TEXTER" COMPETITION?
AND THAT WAS BACK WHEN CELLPHONES ONLY HAD NUMERIC KEYBOARDS.

WOW, ANAI, IS THAT A NEW SHIRT?

TAKA
TAKA
NO.

PØRKATSU
PASSWORD
HUH. PRETTY COOL.
TAKA
TAKA
TAKA

"THE PLAN IS SIMPLE.
"THE EMAIL HAS ALREADY BEEN SENT.
TAKA TAKA TAKA TAKA
COPY
"SENDING IT AGAIN WILL BUMP IT UP TO THE TOP OF THE INBOX... BUT..."
CLCK
CLICK
CLCK

RIIIING
THAT SOUNDS URGENT. MAYBE WE SHOULD ALL BE CHECKING OUR PHONE MESSAGES?
MIGHT BE *SOMETHING IMPORTANT* THERE?

WELL, *UM*--

THAT'S AN IDEA!

A VERY ***BAD*** IDEA IF WE WANT TO MAINTAIN OUR MINDFULNESS! IF WE ALL LOOK AT OUR PHONES NOW, WE WON'T BE MINDING THE PRESENT MOMENT, NOW WILL WE, MY BOY?

MISS GORI, PLEASE CONTINUE. I WAS ***SO*** ENJOYING YOUR DEEP DIVE INTO SERIF FONTS...

"...SENDING IT HUNDREDS OF TIMES..."

...WILL MARK ANY OF ANAI'S EMAILS AS SUSPICIOUS AND MOVE THEM TO SPAM.
DAMN. YOU ACTUALLY DID IT.
ALL RIGHT, PACK IT IN.
FENNEKO? WHAT ARE YOU DOING?
FENNEKO! SOMEONE'S COMING! GET OUT OF THERE!
FENNEKO!
AHA!!

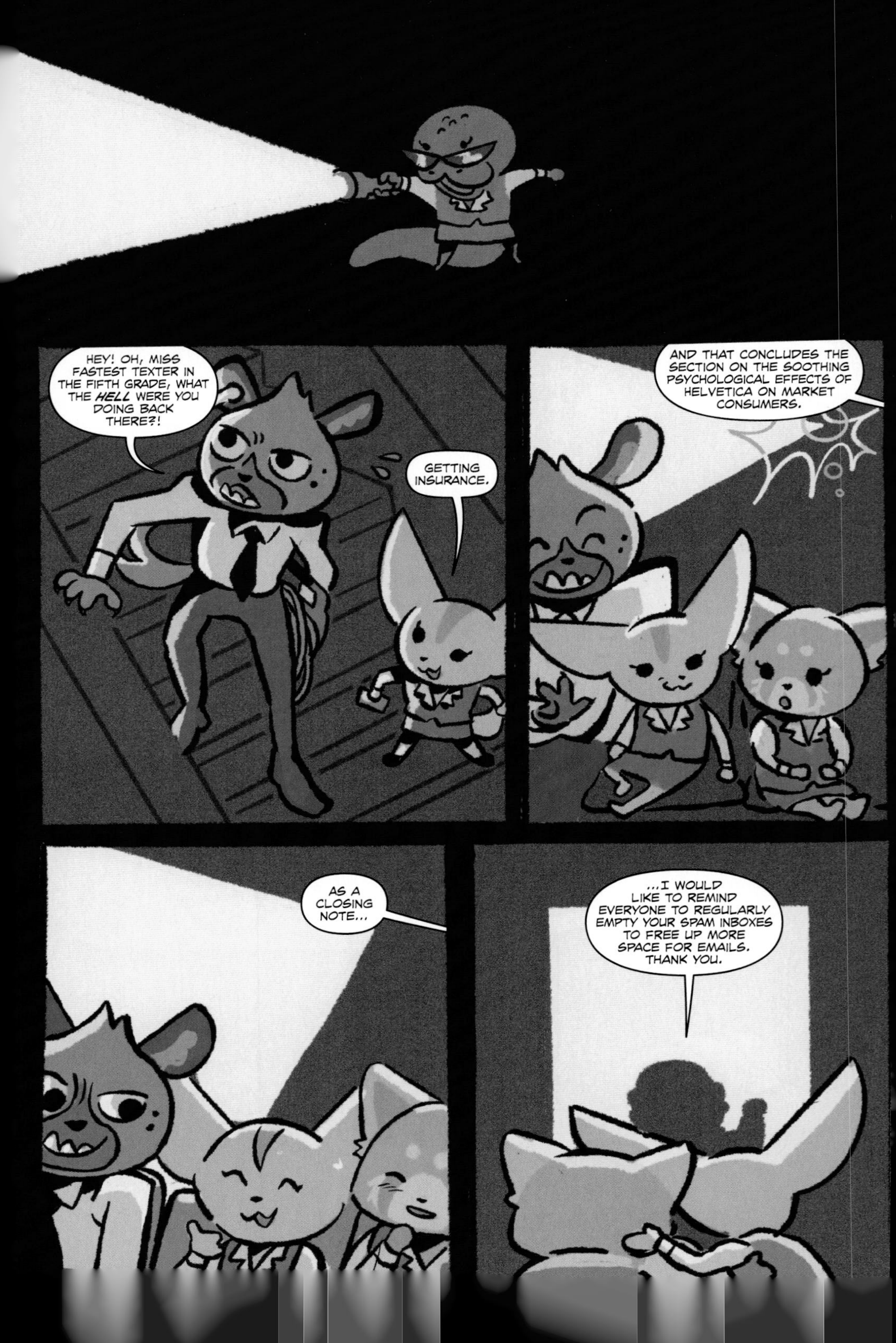
HEY! OH, MISS FASTEST TEXTER IN THE FIFTH GRADE, WHAT THE HELL WERE YOU DOING BACK THERE?!
GETTING INSURANCE.
AND THAT CONCLUDES THE SECTION ON THE SOOTHING PSYCHOLOGICAL EFFECTS OF HELVETICA ON MARKET CONSUMERS.
AS A CLOSING NOTE...
...I WOULD LIKE TO REMIND EVERYONE TO REGULARLY EMPTY YOUR SPAM INBOXES TO FREE UP MORE SPACE FOR EMAILS. THANK YOU.

LATER THAT AFTERNOON, AFTER THE ELECTRICITY CAME BACK ON...
DRINKS SOON! RETSUKO SAYS SHE'LL GET THE FIRST ROUND!
MM-HM. BE THERE IN A SECOND.
URGENT: VIEW ASAP
HM?
CLICK
I downloaded a Time Tracker app onto your computer that will email me periodic updates of whatever videos you're watching, rounds of solitaire you're playing, or whatever else you're doing on there. What you do is none of my business, but if you ever try to get my friend fired over a stupid SnipSnap video again, I will personally email the evidence of your laziness to every potential employer you will ever have from now until your retirement.
All the best,
Fenneko

HAHA
HAHA
HAHA
HAHAHAHAHAHAHA
-fin-

BALLROOM
IS IT LEGAL FOR OUR COMPANY TO DEMAND WE GO TO A FUNDRAISER?
THAT'S CRAZY TALK. THIS IS GREAT.
I'M PSYCHED TO SPEND SATURDAY NIGHT COMPLETELY ON EDGE, SURROUNDED BY A DOZEN PEOPLE WHO COULD FIRE ME.
THAT'S WHY I BROUGHT MY BIGGEST BAG AND A WEEK'S WORTH OF BENTO BOXES.
I PLAN TO TAKE SO MANY APPETIZERS THEY DECIDE IT'S FINANCIALLY IRRESPONSIBLE TO EVER DRAG UNDERPAID UNDERLINGS HERE AGAIN.
AALENDAAAAR!
I'VE GOT A JOB FOR YOU!
UM... NOW? BUT IT'S THE WEEKEND--
AND A WORK EVENT! SO I'M WITHIN MY RIGHTS AS YOUR BOSS TO PUT YOU TO WORK!

HAVE YOU SEEN THE *SILENT AUCTION?!*
I... DOUBT I CAN OUTBID THE CLIENTS, SO I DIDN'T EVEN--
BECAUSE I WILL *NOT LOSE* MY CHANCE AT *THIS--*
--A *PRIVATE GAME* WITH A *CHAMPION GOLF PRO!!*
OKAY...
BUT WHAT DID YOU MEAN ABOUT PUTTING ME TO WORK?
AH. SEE, I PUT IN MY *BID--*
--BUT *YOU* ARE GOING TO SPEND *ALL NIGHT* WATCHING THAT PAPER TO MAKE SURE NO ONE OUTBIDS ME!
MY WIFE WOULD KILL ME IF I *WASTED* A WHOLE SATURDAY OVER HERE. BUT LUCKILY, YOU'RE *TOTALLY ALONE!*
PLUS, THE APPETIZERS LOOKED *GREAT*, BUT THEY KEEP *DISAPPEARING* BEFORE THEY MAKE IT OVER HERE!
ENJOY YOUR NIGHT!

THE GOLF BETWEEN US

CAAALENDAAAR!
MR. TON? I'M ALMOST DONE WITH THOSE BALANCE REPORTS, BUT THERE WAS A REFERENCE TO A CONTRACT ADDENDUM THAT WASN'T INCLUDED--
THAT'S NOT WHY YOU'RE HERE!
THIS IS ABOUT *YOU* WASTING *THREE WEEKS'* WORTH OF MY *SALARY* AT THE FUNDRAISER!!
WHAT?! I'M SORRY, MR. TON, BUT--
--BUT YOU *TOLD* ME TO KEEP BIDDING ON THE GOLF PRO, RIGHT?
THERE WERE *TWO* GOLF PRO AUCTIONS!
ONE WITH *KIN*, THE *GREATEST* LIVING MAN TO PLAY THE GAME...
...AND ONE WITH... SOME *WOMAN!!*
I'M *LUCKY* NO ONE ELSE *TOUCHED* MY... *ENTHUSIASTIC* INITIAL BID ON KIN--
--BECAUSE *YOU* KEPT BIDDING *UP* ON THIS *WOMAN* EVEN *HIGHER!*

WELL... IF OTHER PEOPLE BID THAT MUCH, SHE MUST BE PRETTY GOOD, RIGHT?
AND... NOW YOU GET LESSONS FROM TWO PROS?
IS THAT A JOKE, CALENDAR?
WOMEN AREN'T REAL ATHLETES!
BUT THERE IS A BRIGHT SIDE...
...I'M PLANNING TO MAKE THIS WORTH MY MONEY!
YOU'LL GOLF WITH THIS WOMAN.
AND YOU'LL TRY YOUR BEST.
BECAUSE THERE'S GONNA BE A WAGER ON THE LINE!
IF YOU AND THIS LADY PRO WIN, I'LL APOLOGIZE. AND I WON'T EVEN MAKE YOU PAY ME BACK.
BUT IF THE MEN WIN, YOU'LL HAVE TO WORK OFF THAT DEBT...
...BY POLISHING MY CLUBS EVERY WEEK FOR THE NEXT FIVE YEARS!!

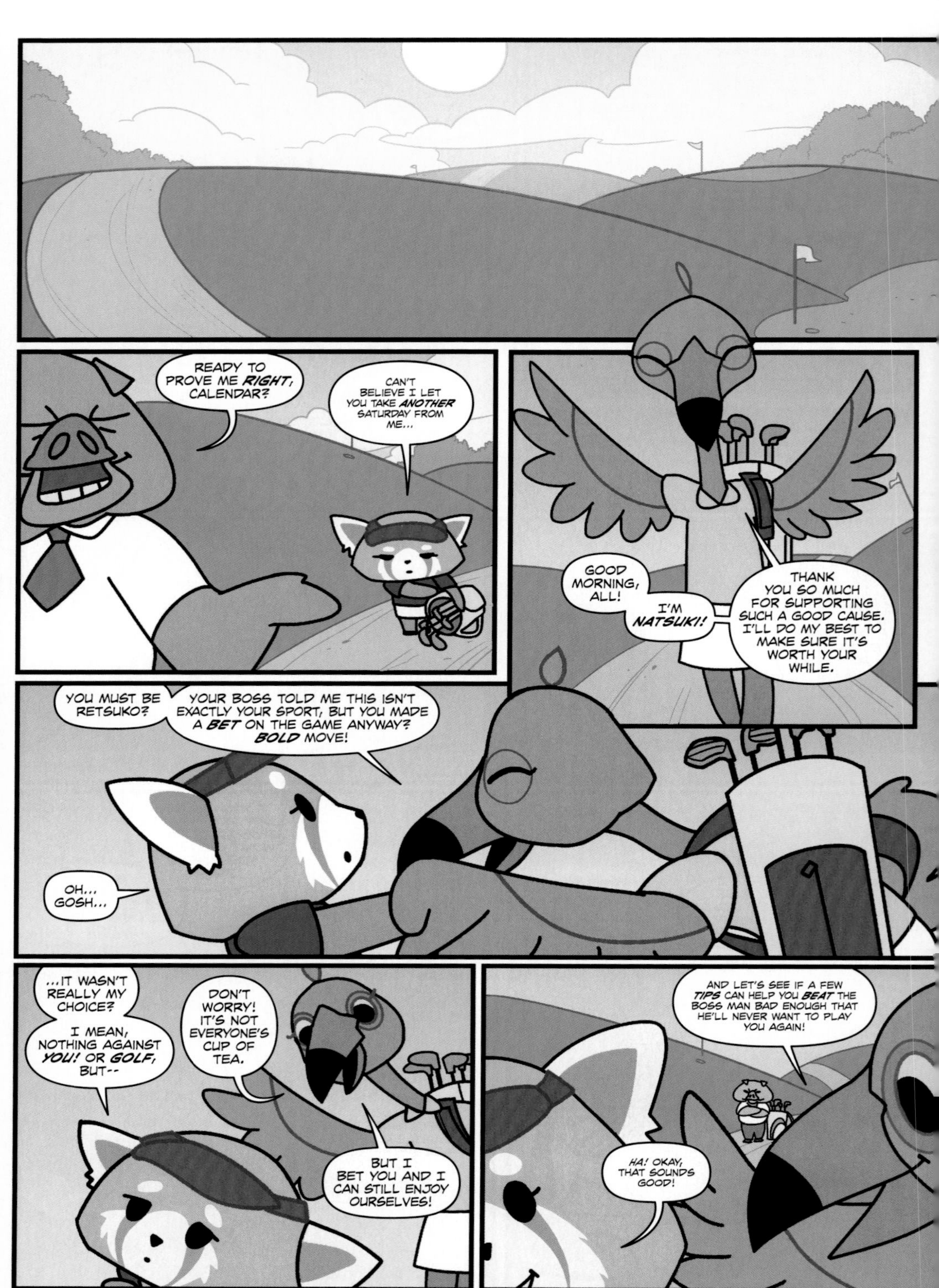
READY TO PROVE ME RIGHT, CALENDAR?
CAN'T BELIEVE I LET YOU TAKE ANOTHER SATURDAY FROM ME...
GOOD MORNING, ALL!
I'M NATSUKI!
THANK YOU SO MUCH FOR SUPPORTING SUCH A GOOD CAUSE. I'LL DO MY BEST TO MAKE SURE IT'S WORTH YOUR WHILE.
YOU MUST BE RETSUKO?
YOUR BOSS TOLD ME THIS ISN'T EXACTLY YOUR SPORT, BUT YOU MADE A BET ON THE GAME ANYWAY? BOLD MOVE!
OH... GOSH...
...IT WASN'T REALLY MY CHOICE?
I MEAN, NOTHING AGAINST YOU! OR GOLF, BUT--
DON'T WORRY! IT'S NOT EVERYONE'S CUP OF TEA.
BUT I BET YOU AND I CAN STILL ENJOY OURSELVES!
AND LET'S SEE IF A FEW TIPS CAN HELP YOU BEAT THE BOSS MAN BAD ENOUGH THAT HE'LL NEVER WANT TO PLAY YOU AGAIN!
HA! OKAY, THAT SOUNDS GOOD!

SO... WHICH ONE OF YOU JUST LIGHTENED MY TAXES BY BIDDING ON THIS DONATION?
I'LL GO A LITTLE EASIER ON YOU...
ME, SIR! I'M... EH...
TON, RIGHT?
YES! COULDN'T THINK OF IT THERE FOR A SECOND!
TOO BAD. HOPED I'D GIVE SOME UP CLOSE AND PERSONAL LESSONS TO THAT LITTLE FEMALE.
WORK ON HER FORM, Y'KNOW WHAT I MEAN?
BUT CALL ME KIN. YOU PAID FOR IT.
THOUGH MAYBE NOT ENOUGH. HOW THE HELL DID NATSUKI GO FOR MORE THAN ME AT THAT AUCTION?!
OH... THAT'S RETSUKO'S FAULT.
WOMEN AREN'T AS CAREFUL WHEN THEY'RE SPENDING OUR MONEY, RIGHT?
SO WHO IS SHE? YOUR GIRLFRIEND?
WHAT?! NO. I'M MARRIED.
SORRY TO HEAR THAT. SO SHE'S YOUR MISTRESS?
NO!
SHE WORKS IN MY OFFICE! UNDER ME.
HA! OKAY, I GET IT.
BUT THERE'S NO REASON WE CAN'T HAVE SOME REAL TALK LIKE REAL MEN. RIGHT, "BOSS"?

LADIES FIRST?
AFTER ALL, SHE'S GONNA NEED THE EXTRA SHOTS!
TMP
OKAY, OKAY, NOT BAD FOR A FEMALE--BUT THIS FIRST HOLE IS FAMOUSLY EASY.
WATCH!
TUNP
SEE, DON'T LISTEN TO NATSUKI--THAT'S HOW YOU WANT TO DO IT, LITTLE LADY.
WELL, THAT WAS GOOD, BUT...
...DIDN'T BOTH OF YOUR SHOTS LAND AT THE GREEN?
IF ANYTHING, HERS WENT A LITTLE FURTHER--
WELL THEN, I GUESS WOMEN HAVE EYESIGHT AS WEAK AS EVERYTHING ELSE!
!
FUFF
MY SHOT WAS OBVIOUSLY MUCH MORE DELIBERATE AND ON-TARGET!

STNK

REEETSUKO!!
YOU BLABBERING FOOL! DON'T EVEN KNOW TO KEEP YOUR MOUTH SHUT ON SOMEONE ELSE'S TEEEE?!

IT WAS *KIN* WHO YELLED, MR. TON.
SO UNLESS YOU WANT TO SHOUT THE SAME AT *HIM*, WE SHOULD JUST LET RETSUKO HERE TAKE HER APPROACH.

SWSSH

PFFT! THAT'S GOTTA BE EMBARRASSING, "BOSS."
HEY-- GRAB MY CLUBS.
LOOK AT THAT, RETSUKO! YOU'RE A NATURAL!

11
11
15
16
C'MON, AMATEUR-- DON'T JUST SWING THIS TIME, *THINK.*
ACCOUNT FOR THE *WIND!*
I'M AN *ACCOUNTANT.* I CAN CALCULATE LONG-TERM COMPOUND INTEREST AND THE IMPACT OF DEPRECIATION PROJECTIONS--
--NOT HOW TO ANGLE DIFFERENTLY FOR *WIND!*
THEN DON'T WORRY ABOUT ANGLE-- JUST MAKE SURE YOU DRIVE ENOUG *POWER* TO KEEP I *STRAIGHT!*
+2 stroke penalty!
SO... SHOULD I HIT HARDER? BECAUSE OF THE WIND?
THERE'S NO CLOCK RUNNING, RETSUKO.
IF CONDITIONS AREN'T RIGHT TO MOVE ON, YOU COULD JUST... WAIT.
OH... REALLY?! THAT SOUNDS... NICE.

GOLF IS WAR!
YOU SHOOT, ADVANCE, AND TAKE NO PRISONERS!
GOLF IS THE PEACEFUL SPORT.
YOU DON'T SCORE BY PUSHING BACK AGAINST AN OPPONENT.
YOU SUCCEED THROUGH FOCUS AND CONTROL AS YOU NAVIGATE NATURE.
25
24
38
35
IT'S ABOUT DOMINATING YOUR COMPETITION, TON!
ESPECIALLY IF YOU'RE GOLFING FOR BUSINESS!
HA. THAT'S FUNNY--
--BECAUSE OUR CEO DEMANDED TON LOSE WHEN HE PLAYED A CLIENT.
CAAALENDAR!
HAR HAR! IS THAT TRUE?!
I'D NEVER LET MYSELF BE EMASCULATED LIKE THAT!

38
35
53
51
HMMM...
OHH--TOO BAD, SWEETHEART!
I COULD TELL FROM OUR DRIVES THAT MINE LANDED HERE.
SO YOURS MUST HAVE GONE IN THE DRINK.

OH... I GUESS SO?
HA. GUESS MY "BEGINNER'S LUCK" HAD TO RUN OUT SOMETIME, RIGHT?
HOLD ON.
AH. HERE WE ARE...

HERE'S THE BALL.
AND YOU STILL PLAY WITH CUSTOMS, RIGHT, KIN?
SO THE BALL--AND THE TWO-STROKE PENALTY--ARE YOURS.
WOMEN, RIGHT?
HATE TO HAVE 'EM RUINING THE GAME...
...BUT DON'T MIND WATCHING 'EM!
WHAT?
I'M JUST SAYIN' WHAT EVERY GUY THINKS!

YOU CAN SPEAK FOR YOURSELF...
...BUT I DON'T FEEL THE SAME.

WHAT?
OH, RIGHT. PROBABLY GOTTA COVER YOUR ASS WITH THIS ONE, *EH,* "BOSS"?
NO... I MEAN IT.

WHEN RETSUKO BID ON A DAY WITH NATSUKI, I *WAS* UPSET...
...UNTIL I THOUGHT ABOUT BRINGING MY *DAUGHTERS.*

"THE WHOLE RIDE HOME, AND ALL NIGHT, I REALIZED I WAS GETTING MORE AND MORE *HOPEFUL* AND *EXCITED* THAT MAYBE *THEY'D* GET INTO GOLF, TOO!
"THAT MAYBE MY GIRLS AND I WOULD FINALLY HAVE SOMETHING WE COULD *SHARE* AND... *BOND* OVER?"

BUT WHEN I BROUGHT UP THE IDEA AT BREAKFAST, THEY *HATED* THE IDEA.
THEY JUST KEPT MOCKING GOLF, HOW "BORING" IT IS...
...AND THE IDEA OF SPENDING TIME WITH THEIR "BORING" DAD.

BUT I STILL WISH THEY COULD BE HERE.
THAT I COULD SHARE THIS WITH THEM.

PFFFT! THAT'S STUPID.
GIRLS HAVE NO PLACE IN REAL SPORTS.
IF I WERE YOU, I'D JUST WORRY ABOUT MARRYING THEM OFF--
--LET THEM BE A PAIN IN SOME OTHER GUYS' ASSES!

YOU DON'T HAVE A FAMILY. AND IF YOU DID--
I HAVE TWO EX-WIVES. THAT'S BAD ENOUGH!
IF YOU DID HAVE KIDS, IT MIGHT OPEN YOUR EYES.
YOU'D BE SURPRISED HOW SOMEONE YOU SAW AS SMALL AND HELPLESS CAN PROVE TO BE STRONGER, SMARTER, AND MORE AMAZING THAN YOU EVER WOULD HAVE GUESSED.
YOU MIGHT START TO EXPECT PEOPLE COULD BE MORE THAN THEY'VE SHOWN YOU...
...INSTEAD OF ASSUMING THEM TO BE LESS.
HA.
SORRY, "BOSS." MAYBE YOUR GIRLS DUPED YOU INTO THIS "FEMALES CAN DO ANYTHING A MAN CAN" CRAP...
...BUT THE REST OF US LIVE ON PLANET EARTH. WHERE MEN RUN EVERYTHING AND GET THE GLORY, BECAUSE WE'RE JUST BETTER.
ALL RIGHT...
I SEE SOME FOOLS JUST WON'T LEARN UNLESS YOU TEACH 'EM LOUD.

A MAN SHOULDN'T NEED A DAUGHTER, MOM, OR A WIFE
TO HAVE BASIC RESPECT FOR OTHER HUMAN LIFE
I LIKE TO BUST CHOPS, BUT YOU TAKE IT TOO FAR
DRAG A SUCKA OVER WHAT THEY DO, NOT
WHO THEY ARE

INSTEAD, YOU'RE AN OVERPAID, ENTITLED PUNK
WHO SOMEHOW THINKS NO ONE CAN GOLF WITHOUT
MAN-JUNK!
YOU'RE NOT SOME HARD-FIGHTIN', MACHO MAN DEFENDING A FLAG
YOUR WORK'S A LIGHT WALK WHILE SOMEONE
CARRIES YOUR BAGS!
EVERY WOMAN THAT I KNOW HUSTLES HARDER THAN YOU
YOU COULDN'T WALK AN EIGHTH OF A MILE IN THEIR SHOES!
IF YOU WOKE UP TOMORROW, AND SOCIETY SWITCHED
THE WORLD WOULD DROP YOUR LAZY, WHINY ASS
IN A DITCH!

YOU DONE, AMATEUR?
BECAUSE I DON'T CARE WHAT YOU FEEL.
RIGHT NOW, MY ONLY CONCERN IS MY OWN BET!
SO GET YOUR HEAD IN THE GAME AND START PULLING YOUR WEIGHT...
"...OR I'M GONNA BE OUT BIG MONEY TO THAT PINK WITCH!
"THE ONLY THING WORSE--
"--WILL BE THE INDIGNITY OF LOSING TO WOMEN!!
"IMAGINE WHAT SHE'LL SAY ABOUT YOU AT WORK!
"WHAT KIND OF MAN THEY'LL THINK YOU ARE..."
WHAM

+2 stroke penalty!
DOOOOSH
OOPS.
NO WAY TO WIN IT NOW.
GUESS THE WOMEN JUST PLAYED BETTER THAN US TODAY.
ARE YOU FREAKING KIDDING ME, TON?!
FORGET IT! THE BET'S OFF!!
THIS... THIS WAS A SETUP THE WHOLE TIME!
AND-- AND--I WAS GOING EASY ON YOU ALL!
BUT YOU FEMALES HAD TO GO AND CHEAT!
I'M GONNA WARN EVERY GUY IN THE CLUBHOUSE ABOUT YOU THREE!
I-- I BET YOU MESSED WITH MY CLUBS, TOO!
I WOULDN'T MAKE MORE BETS YOU CAN'T WIN, KIN.
BUT THIS TANTRUM YOU'RE THROWING IS ENOUGH OF A PRIZE FOR ME.

NOK NOK NOK
DIRECTOR TON... SIR?
I... I WANTED TO APOLOGIZE FOR... FOR RUINING YOUR TIME WITH... A MAN YOU ADMIRE.
NAH. HE'S NOTHING SPECIAL.
YOU AND NATSUKI ARE BETTER MEN THAN HE'LL EVER BE.
UH... THANK YOU?
JUST SO WE'RE CLEAR--I LOST ON PURPOSE.
SO YOU DIDN'T REALLY WIN THE BET, CALENDAR.
BUT... IT'S ALSO NOT RIGHT TO MAKE YOU POLISH MY CLUBS.
YOU ARE GOING TO DO THESE EXTRA REVIEWS, THOUGH.
BUT THAT'S ONLY BECAUSE I KNOW YOU CAN HANDLE IT.

The End

Aggretsuko™

bonus materials

CHARACTER DESIGNS

BY Lisa DuBois

HOT GIRL SNOW LEOPARD

WITCH OWL

OLD YOGI IBEX

MA N' PA PROTEIN

COVER GALLERY

#1 VARIANT COVER

BY CASSIE ANDERSON

#1 VARIANT COVER

BY GEORGE CALTSUDOUS

#2 VARIANT COVER

BY ARIELLE JOVELLANOS

#3 VARIANT COVER

BY SHADIA AMIN

READ MORE FROM ONI PRESS!

AGGRETSUKO: METAL TO THE MAX
By Daniel Barnes, D.J. Kirkland, Jarrett Williams, and Brenda Hickey
Retsuko, the highly-relatable red panda and star of Sanrio's *Aggretsuko*, stars in three all-new comic tales of office madness!

AGGRETSUKO: STRESS MANAGEMENT
By Michelle Gish, Sarah Stern, Daniel Barnes, Patabot, Shadia Amin, and D.J. Kirkland
Collecting issues #4–6 of the hit comic series, find out what happens when a workaholic has to take a break—literally?! And when the entire office is forced into an interoffice sports competition, who will get the gold?!

MOONCAKES
By Suzanne Walker and Wendy Xu
A story of love and demons, family and witchcraft.

ARCHIVAL QUALITY
By Ivy Noelle Weir and Steenz
An evocative ghost story exploring trauma and mental health.

DREAM DADDY: A DAD DATING COMIC BOOK
By Various
Oni Press presents Dream Daddy, a comics series based on the acclaimed Game Grumps visual novel video game!

BLACK MAGE
By Daniel Barnes and D.J. Kirkland
When a historically white wizarding school opens its doors to its first-ever black student, everyone believes that the wizarding community is finally taking its first crucial steps toward inclusivity. Or is it?

For more information on these and other fine Oni Press comic books and graphic novels, visit www.onipress.com.